TH... N...

CONST...

A Guide for Y...
Their

ers to

ecrets

ution

CREATING THE C

PREAMBLE -

BILL OF RIGHTS

BRANCHES O

CHECKS AND BAL

AMENDMENTS

And guess what, M

thrilling and importar

ones!

Why grasping the (
for children and Mc

Picture the US Cons

that keeps our natio

like a treasure map

shows us how our la

made, and how fairn

bird? Or the right

aching for the sun?

at the Constitution

and children alike

Mom and Dad, you
know how to teach
your little ones to be
responsible and
kind? Well,
understanding the
Constitution is

Learning Together

everyone, young on

When you embark o

oh, what outstanding

newfound wonders y

can amaze your pal

and Mom and Dads

magnificent voyage
to the realm of the
s Constitution – a
ystical guidebook
at weaves the fabric
our land as
acefully as a
bbling brook.

we delve into the
itution" and grasp
ed treasure.

n as a grand set of

...cellent harmony
-in our grand United
es.

te our musings,
 enrich our nation.

anting guide,
e riddles concealed

up for a voyage of
ng – a journey that
ful bedrock of our

Who were the Four

Close your eyes and
individuals who lived
different time. These
Founding Fathers. T
their era, charting a
remarkable land.

Among these illustrio
echo in the halls of h
Thomas Jefferson, B
Alexander Hamilton,

sed their wisdom
nd imagination to
onstruct a nation
nd a government
ntirely from scratch!

vhere people could
 themselves, and
 of their lives.

hat would have
stifled people's
o create a system
ould be heard, and
reality through a

John Adams: A ferv

chapter, we have

nd their remarkable

d States

The Constitutional

Imagine, if you will, a
minds, all in one roo
wizards in a hidden
the Constitutional Co
purpose.

You see, after our co
Britain, it was like we
pieces. So, the wise
Philadelphia in 1787
improve our governr

let's talk about this

ificent Constitution.

bit like a treasure

hat guides our

nment's journey.

nost enchanting

It divides the

nment into three

hes, like three

erful friends

ng together.

president as the

captain of a ship.

wed and steer the

These three branche
clock, each with its c
harmoniously to kee
smoothly.

Comparing the Co

Imagine you're build
special plan, right? \
very plan, but for ou
rules, shows who's i
can live together in f

of the Constitutional
es of government,
 a magical
 the U.S.
nore stunning rules
al.

Breaking down the

Imagine, if you will, t
opening spell in a fai
to the Constitution, a
country was created

Now, let's take those
them down into simp

• protecting a city

mote the General
lfare: Think of this
saying, "Let's make
e everyone is happy
l healthy, like
ping your friends
en they need it."

cure the Blessings
Liberty: This is
ut ensuring we can
by our freedoms,
exploring a magical

characters in our fav

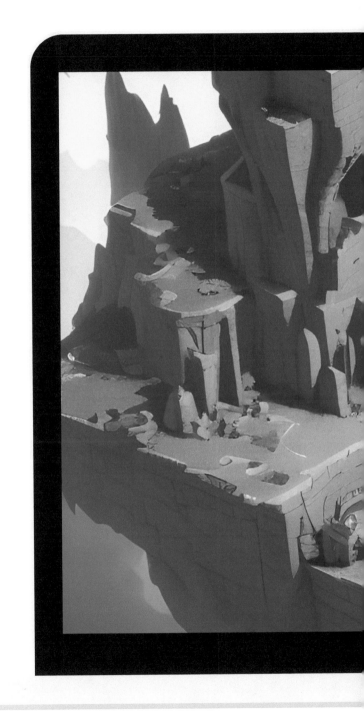

"Ensuring Domest

. Constitution, we'll
me the heart and

s adventure has

and discovery!

**Explaining the first[...]
friendly way:**

Imagine, if you will, t[...]
magical shield that p[...]

It lists ten important [...]
freedom and fairnes[...]
favorite stories.

*Amendment 1: Fre[...]
of Speech:* We all h[...]
the right to say what[...]
think, just lik[...] shar[...]

t says, "Our home,

houses and how the
henever it wants,
 strangers
means that the
ldiers stay in your
 war going on.

One smart fella
named Justice
William O. Douglas
said it best: "The

Amendment 4: Sea

as our privacy rule, s
through or take our t
seizure

rial: This is like

urt gets a fair and

n a mystery solving

Trial: Think of this

a group of wise

e're right or wrong,

ame.

nusual

nobody can be

, just like the good

ce cruel

Freedom of speech

Now, let's explore so

Freedom of Speech

thoughts and ideas,
their minds. It's like .
with your friends wit

Freedom of Religio

favorite magical wor
your gods or goddes
characters in a fairy
adventures.

this enchanting

ogether and

agine, if you will, a
itastic treehouse
ep in the heart of
 enchanted forest.
is treehouse
presents our gover-
ient, and it's divided
o three magical
oms, each belong-
g to one of the
anches:

referees in a game,
rules. If someone thi
come to this room, a
decide what's right.

But here's the magic
rooms aren't separa
all connected by sec
passages and hidde
This means they hav
together, a bit like ch
in a grand adventure
helping each other.

Fun scenarios that
how each branch o

on.

 our government
ings are fair,
 o one gets too

 ms and Dads in

'round the campfire
this enchanting adve

he importance of

Settling a Disagree

a story arguing abou

cake. They go to cou

the judges listen car

the judges ensure th

fight, they share it.

These examples sho

how each branch of

our government has

f the Judicial

carefully, one

resolve their

we grow and change
thrilling adventure to

Understanding the Constitution:

Imagine, if you will, c
storybook with its ow
want to add a new a
in the story?

That's where amend
adding new pages o
keep it fresh and fair

s of the story to

Bill of Rights:

Now, let's explore
chapters in our Co

adventures, adding

our grand story of

Moms and Dads, in

magnificent Constitu

today!

Linking history to t

ntemporary
itution plays its

Now, let's dive into

kids like you who s

Tinker v. Des Moin

erful Moms and

It's like discovering a
and we're going to e
can stay engaged w
Let's embark on this

**Encouraging kids a
stay engaged with**

racters in a Karen
h friends, read the
s what you find.

ink of it as a grand
poppers Day." On
ay the Constitution
n!

**Now, let's discover
help you on your C**

Books: Imagine a lil
Constitution. There a

haracters in an
quest:

n a grand
for or against a
ndly debate, and it
erspectives.

onsider this as
eate a mini-
ool. Decide on rules
how they work

1. Making Our Vote

Our votes are like th
leaders. We must m
honestly and counte

m

what they believe

ideas:

No More Risky Vot
voting methods that
safe. Let's stick to w

Stop Fake Ballots:
be faked. Each state
place to keep our vo

The Election Integr
special team called t
They're like the supe
us innovative ideas a
equipment and rules

scovering the US

thrilling
of words and ideas.
's secrets, learned
heir wisdom, and
oday.

Inspiring kids to be

Imagine yourselves
your powers for goo
citizen means you c
country, like the her
stand up for what's

about the
know with others.
p so they can

es, ready to use
ctive and informed
ur community and
dmired stories who

Three Branches: O
the Executive Branc
Branch (like the dec
Branch (like the rule

government has
ss), Legislative
dicial (like the rule

dments to the
st like a shield

Kids' Rights: Just li
heroes in tales, kids
rights too, like the rig
learn, speak up, and

a magical key to
nd becoming a
r. Use it to explore,
knowledge and

oms and Dads, as
ough the U.S.
re now equipped
that can shape

pters of fun and
ou. Discover the
nd secrets that make
anding the land of the
dy to unlock the USA
itution!

THOR

Printed in the USA
CPSIA information can be obtained
at www.ICGtesting.com
LVHW070443101123
763485LV00053B/1311